PROBING THE DARKNESS FOR THE LIGHT

PROBING THE DARKNESS FOR THE LIGHT

POEMS

JOAN PROVENCHER

FULMEN PRESS
BERKELEY, CA

2013 FULMEN PRESS Paperback Edition

ISBN 978-0-9896796-0-2
1.Poetry. I. Title.

Published in the United States by Fulmen Press

Library of Congress Control Number: 2013912475
Joan Provencher, Berkeley, CA

CONTENTS

CONTENTS

PROBING
THE
DARKNESS
FOR
THE LIGHT

One touch of nature makes
the whole world kin

William Shakespeare

ANOINTED BY AN ETHEREAL SPIRIT

TIGER BUTTERFLIES floating on air
Separating, coming together,
Spiraling heavenward and then appearing
as leaves falling to earth.

STANDING STILL AS A STATUE, totally in awe,
I was courted by a Tiger Swallow Tail Butterfly.
Flying into my face almost landing on my nose,
Then veering around my head an inch away.

REPEATEDLY LEAVING AND RETURNING TO TAUNT , to
play, to explore.

WHAT CAN I SAY. I am so deeply affected, so
enamored by this joyful being.

THIS ETHEREAL SPIRIT has touched my Soul.

AWAKENING

ARROWS PIERCE MY HEART

SORROW, HEARTBREAK

LIFE IS AWAKENING

A TORRENT OF WITHHELD MOTIONS

AND EMOTIONS EXPLODE THE DAM

OF CONTROLS

TEARS FLOOD THE PLANE OF MY

EXISTENCE QUICKENING AND

REJUVENATING THE LIFE FORCE WITHIN

Reunited

In the deep dark forest a red bird with
violet wings sang a deeply touching
melodious song of its deep felt love

A blue bird with yellow wings heart opening
to its lover's call burst into song

In the darkness they had forgotten their love
shadows of life had intruded

White blazing light burst forth making
the forest radiant
Love had returned, life was flowing

Joyous celebrations ensued

a winter stroll

the dark cloud-ladened sky casts its shadow,
the lake appears silky black

the bay sandwiched between two points moves rhythmically
as the waves wash up onto its icy shores

rocks littered with ice crystals shine like diamonds resurrected
from the depths of the lake, a treasure trove below the silky black
surface.

the winter cold has transformed the body of water into a mixture of
ice shards of various sizes, a precursor to a frozen lake.

as waves wash up over the ice covered rocks on shore,
the chiming of ice pieces cascading off the icy rocks sounds a
symphony of nature

Changes

life is changing

seams are breaking

energy flowing

where am I going?

flowing in the river

heading for the sea of life.

ever churning - don't know where I am

going.

matters not - I am alive

vibrating with life

7

Sanctuary

sunlight dances on the endless ocean
waves stretching to the horizon.

overhead seagulls sail by in the clear blue
skies while dolphins frolic in the surf

waves endlessly reach to touch the beach
on which sandpipers and other shorebirds
are searching for sustenance

in a grass hut looking out to this wonder
furnished with a sumptuous bed and hot
tub i merge into all that surrounds one
into relaxation, comfort, and the bliss of
the moment

my escape into another world
a dream world in my waking hours
to relax, refresh, and to center

Conditionings

everything we do
conditions us

be different

do different things

do what you love

be strong

be loving

be gentle

9

NO EXCUSES

I have made my choices,
sometimes feeling a need
for excuses.
In all honesty knowing
the way of life,
why the excuses?

Living is living,
not right or wrong,
not about me,
not about you.

Let go of the grief,
let go of the sadness,
let go of this madness.

The Fall

pinnacles rising, eagles soaring,
lizards scampering.
clear blue skies, hard rock, a willing partner.
joy and freedom preside.

donning rock shoes, rope and hardware,
we set up to ascend.

passionate, burying recent emotional trauma,
i climb quickly. it will be dark soon.

i decide not to take the usual precautions.
"forget the protection. i have never fallen.
this is not a difficult climb".

at thirty-two feet I edge my toe into a crack,
i shift my weight onto my toe,
it slips out, the crack is slimy.
falling , my voice expresses itself, two short
syllables.
totally in the moment the outcome unknown.

at twenty feet I hit a ledge, i feel the hardness
of the rock, my ankle breaks.

now i am head first, my body shifts.
I hit the deck, landing on my right side in an
area devoid of rocks. i am alive.

SNOW QUEEN

SHOWER OF GLITTERING SNOW CRYSTALS FALLING ONTO MY FACE
THE SUN SHINING BRIGHTLY
SNOW GEESE HONKING OVERHEAD
A DREAMY WORLD. I AM TRANSFIXED.

INSIDE MY HEART ENERGY SWIRLING AND VIBRATING WITH ANTICIPATION AND EXCITEMENT
FOR THE DAY THAT LAY AHEAD,
I WILL MEET THE SNOW QUEEN IN THE LAND OF ICE CRYSTALS.
MY ARRIVAL WILL NATURALLY COINCIDE AT THE TIME THE LAST SNOW CRYSTAL LANDS
UPON MY FACE.

I AM TAKEN ABACK WHEN I GLIMPSE THE CRYSTALLINE ICE DOME,
THE ABODE OF THE SNOW QUEEN
SURROUNDED BY MAGNIFICENT BLUE SPRUCE TREES,
THE ICE DOME REFLECTS COLORS OF THE RAINBOW - PURPLE, VIOLET, BLUE,
GREEN, RED, ORANGE, AND YELLOW.
FROLICKING IN THE SNOW ARE THE LEGENDARY SIBERIAN SILVER GRAY WOLVES , THE
COMPANIONS OF THE SNOW QUEEN.

ASCENDING THE STAIRS HEWN FROM BLUE SPRUCE, I WAVE MY HAND ACROSS THE
ICICLES TO ANNOUNCE MY ARRIVAL.
A DOOR OPENS AND MY HEART OPENS AS I GAZE INTO THE EYES OF THE SNOW QUEEN.

ALL MY LIFE I HAD FORESEEN THE TIME I WOULD MEET HER AND THE TIME HAD ARRIVED.
WAVES OF LOVE AND GRATITUDE TO MY BELOVED FLOW OVER MY BEING.
MY HEART POUNDING AND THUMPING WITH EXPANDING EXCITEMENT OF AT LONG LAST
HAVING ARRIVED.

SHE OPENS HER ARMS INTO WHICH I FALL.
HER LOVE ENVELOPS MY BEING AND IN THIS UNION I AM TRANSFORMED INTO A BODYLESS
JET OF PURE UNCONTAMINATED UNCONDITIONAL LOVE.
THE STATE LASTS FOR WHAT FEELS LIKE EONS, ALTHOUGH IT LASTS PERHAPS A FEW
SECONDS.

GIVING THANKS AND HEARTFELT GRATITUDE I DEPART IN A SHOWER OF GLITTERING SNOW
CRYSTALS FALLING ONTO MY FACE.

PROBING THE DARKNESS FOR THE LIGHT

THE DARK DEEP VELVET DARKNESS whispers so softly its deep hidden secrets. Murmurings of creation past and present coexist in one voice of the cosmos.

STAGGERING COSMIC FORCES beyond our imagination created a tapestry of forms. Forms emerging out of the deep velvet darkness and then merging back, the eternal cycle of birth and death.

Being born out of the darkness, the WOMB OF LIFE AND LOVE, flowers the multitude, the many forms of creation.

Within this magnificent darkness LIGHT BURSTS FORTH in dazzling colors and shades, in a harmonious coexistence with the darkness.

Looking at the clear sky in the DARKNESS OF THE NIGHT , one sees the pinpoints of light of the macrocosm as the light is perceivable by the microcosm as it enters our orbits.

Reverence of unfathomable depth penetrates my heart, creating deep felt VIBRATIONS OF LOVE, JOY, AND FREEDOM. Gratitude springs forth from my soul to the cosmos, the cradle of all existence.

We are prone to bend head and knee in response to the awe and wonder of this SUBLIME GROUND OF EXISTENCE out of which all creation has issued forth.

MY BELOVED

*My heart resonates its powerful beat
when I think of you my love.*

*I love you - I know I have always loved you.
You have been with me always, even when
I knew you not.*

*When I first met you, I had no idea my love for
you would grow larger than life itself in my heart.*

*Our love started as spontaneous flames of
passion burst forth from our hearts producing
a romantic love so powerful we would say to
one another - you are the love of my life.*

*Our love knows no bounds, it cannot be
contained, it will continue to pour forth and
expand as the years go by.*

BAX KITTY

My little baby
mountain lion, my
little baby cougar,
words I so often
repeated to my
red abyssinian,
Bax Kitty, as she
sat upon my lap
bestowing love
bites to my neck
giving me surges
of joy.

Memories of paws
pattering, paws
galloping, leaps
onto the counter
then the refrig
ending upon a
cabinet close to
the ceiling, a roost from
which she could observe
the comings and goings in
the house which was her world
Using the walls as backboards
she would spring off them totally
changing direction and to my great
surprise pounce on my chest as a jest.

So beautiful, so elegant, so athletic, so
faithful, and so very loving was my amazing
abyssinian named Bax Kitty.

15

Butterflies

BUTTERFLIES FLOATING ON AIR

So delicate, so fragile, so poetic

Just being butterflies

PERHAPS SOMEDAY WE CAN JUST BE HUMANS

DELIGHTING IN BEING

Without all the elements that separate us from one another

The comparisons, competition,
judgements, the images

FRIENDSHIP

OUR SOULS SING SONGS of friendship, for sharing life's longings, life's jubilations, and for sharing life's sorrows which pierce our hearts.

IN COMMUNION with one another, we keep afloat, on the sea of life in its storms and its calm

GIVE WING AND REFUGE to one another, allowing faith in our understanding, hope for peace and harmony, and love to flower in our hearts,

Friendship creates a FOUNTAIN OF EXPANDING LOVE, giving us strength and the will to endure life's purifying ritual, which pulverizes our fragmented beings so that we can be in union with the wholeness of life.

FROST

The cold night has blanketed the earth with
frost
The whiteness covers the green fields and
rests upon rooftops

Bright red/yellow Japanese maple leaves
etched with white dazzling ice crystals

The wetness on the ground has become an
icy crunchy surface to walk upon

As the sun rises the crystalline world fades
into the day

Womb of Life

Darkness, the source and ground of all
existence, envelops my soul,
It nourishes my life, providing new
sprouts for sustenance and growth.

Going into the depth of the darkness,
joy enters my soul and I rejoice.
I dance, I sing songs of new life and
of resurrection,
for a new and glorious moment - a new
day - a new life - a new existence.

Within this magnificent darkness, the
womb of all beginnings and endings,
I connect with the wholeness of life
and experience fireworks exploding
within my heart and soul.

Transfixed in space
surrounded by an eternal
void

Such effort to move –
unless the move has intrinsic
meaning

Meaning to my heart, my
soul, to my innermost being

METAMORPHOSIS

all hands on deck
work to be done
this old boat will sail again
to new horizons
uncharted seas

vitality – passion
power
rebirth
the dragon bursts forth
from the turbulent sea
and flies heavenward

21

BLESSED MOTHER

LIGHT OF MY LIFE,
Your love fills my heart to the brim,
and flows into my daily life
Your love nourishes my heart, it nourishes my soul

IN THE TRIALS AND TRIBULATIONS OF LIFE,
Your love gives one the strength to face
and overcome the challenges of life.
I know that your love is always there for me,
perhaps that is what is meant by amazing grace

LOVE IS AMAZING GRACE
Love is the presence of the divine in our lives

MOTHER, YOU BESTOW THAT AMAZING GRACE,
Which flows from the divine through you
to your children and your friends

Thank you for *THE WONDROUS, MYSTICAL, MIRACLE,*
THE GIFT OF LOVE

BANANA SLUG

It had rained for a week

The woodlands satiated,
exhibit a plethora of new life.

Mushrooms of various shapes, sizes, and colors.
Fungi, delicate as lace, and solid bulky forms
decorate living and dead trees.

One tree - the remaining skeleton - ten feet high,
shares its existence with wafer-thin delicate white and
rust lacy fungi.

Oh my ! a banana slug feasting on the lacy white fungi !

Searching further, four other banana slugs are nestled
between the ridges of the bark.

23

WAKE UP

MOTHER EARTH VIOLATED
SO MANY WAYS
DAY AFTER DAY,

SEEING THE DESTRUCTION OUT OF GREED,
MY HEART SHATTERS
BLOOD OF LIFE POURS FORTH
HEARTACHE, GRIEF, SORROW

LIFE IS SACRED, LIFE IS DIVINE
LIFE IS INTERCONNECTIVENESS
WHERE IS THE REVERENCE?

WE ARE DESTROYING THE CRADLE
OF OUR LIVES, OF ALL LIVING THINGS,
OF ALL EARTHLY EXISTENCE.

RISE UP AND JOIN THE MULTITUDES FIGHTING FOR
OUR BIRTHRIGHT OF AN ENVIRONMENT, A BEING
THAT IS A CLEAN, UNDAMAGED, LIVING ORGANIC
WHOLENESS.

The Forest

Wandering among the trees in the forest I hear the
whisperings and feel the pulsations of the life
surrounding me.

The earths vapors envelop and permeate my being.
The plants, lichens, mushrooms, the animals, and the
insects are vibrating with life.

The pulse of life surges, recedes, surges, and recedes
Like the waves of the ocean on the shores of our lives
Extending forever into eternity.

Sleep

Drifting, drifting off to sleep
Thoughts drifting through my consciousness
Thoughts crisp and clear as the light of day
morphing into fuzzy thinking,
the material of the dream world

Rationality releasing its control

Thoughts drifting - becoming free to wander
unhampered in the waters of our life

THE CLIMB

Climbing on granite, my partner belaying
below began to speak doubts about the route.
Having had a mishap there some years before,
fear and anxiety preside.

Doubts, can you make it to the top of this
climb and not fall?
The belayer is speaking the unspeakable. It's
dangerous.

I am at the halfway point, totally committed.
The climb is protectionless. The only purpose
of the rope is to bring up my partner.

Doubts enter my mind, then fear. My foot is
shaking on its tenuous placement,
sewing machine foot.

My movement is frozen. Is this to be my last
climb? Am I about to become a corpse or a
totally broken human? Thoughts spinning
through my mind.

Suddenly, I gain resolve. I have resurrected faith
in my abilities. As the heavens open I move
skillfully, deliberately, and swiftly to the top of
the climb.

Mirror Lake

AFTER A RELEASE
PEACE
CALM
ALL IS REFLECTED

DIPPING THE OAR INTO THE LAKE,

RIPPLES APPEAR FORMING CONCENTRIC CIRCLES,

SPREADING OUT,
UNTIL THE LAKE IS A MIRROR
PEACE
CALM

Lost Love

My heart laments for lost love tonight
Bonds of a powerful love broken by conditionings
of competition, aggression, and violence, that
human beings are schooled in, which we all have
in our hearts.

Great sorrow pervades my soul
So much healing to be done

The full moon shines brilliantly as
the fog layers pass
The light of the moon will heal me tonight

CHANGES

LIMBO

SHIFTING SANDS

FEELING CHANGE

INNER QUIETNESS

COMING HOME

NO EXCUSES

CHOICES MADE
PRICE PAID
GRIEF AND SADNESS
EGO EVAPORATES
PEACE COMES
A LIFE LIVED

BAX, THE ABYSSINIAN

SO SOFT - THE FUR, THE PURRS, THE LOVE BITES,
THE PATTERING FEET.

SHE TEACHES LIFE, SHE TEACHES UNDERSTANDING,
SHE TEACHES LOVE.

SHE IS AN ABYSSINIAN WORSHIPPED BY THE EGYPTIANS,
WORSHIPPED BY ME.

DARKNESS

darkness envelops my soul giving it
shelter,
allowing it to pour forth its light into
the abyss.

searching the abyss, truth surfaces.
the discovery of the essence and
truth of my existence rekindles
passion within for the sacredness and
the wholeness of life.

time to move on

get out of your stalemate
walls closing in,
life becoming lifeless,
prison walls self-created.
how does this happen?

perception of what is in my
face leaving no trace,
no way out of it but escape

into the sunlight
into the river of life

feel the water
feel the flow
feel the life

Bobcat

Bobcat is wandering in a field of grass, looking about, crouching, waiting
Appears to be hunting Pocket Gopher
There are holes in the grass the right size

At one point Bobcat jams her paw into one of the holes - unsuccessful

Later she crouches, moves forward, and plucks Pocket Gopher out of its hole

Bobcat is now searching for a place to enjoy her dinner

35

MOONRISE

Moonrise over a turbulent sea.
The moonlight penetrates the sea's deep waters.

The seascape is the nature of life, both turbulent and serene.

We all need serenity and turbulence to break out of our shells - to expand, to develop.

I always feel so lost by the gradual letting go of intimate relationship and at the same time scared, in awe, and intrigued by this process of evolution.

The moon, a sense of peace, silence, and acceptance of life is rising over the turbulent sea, over my grief, loss, and struggles to accept life as it is, and its inevitable changes.

RENEWAL

OVERWHELMED BY THE DARKNESS, THE COLD,
AND THE STARKNESS,
MY HEART AND SOUL WANDER THE DRY, ARID
PLAINS SEARCHING FOR LIFE

A GLIMPSE OF TWO BEINGS
ONE HAD TOUCHED THE OTHER WITH
UNFATHOMABLE LOVE AND TENDERNESS

LIGHTNING STRIKES THE STARK PLANE OF MY
EXISTENCE
A TORRENTIAL DOWNPOUR OF LOVE FLOWS AS
MY HEART QUICKENS
MY HEART AND SOUL SPRING TO LIFE

NOTES

The photographs in this book, PROBING THE DARKNESS FOR THE LIGHT, are photos I have taken in the past 12 years with the following exceptions:

COVER PAGE photo: ISON COMET, NASA, www.nasa.gov

PAGE 3, photo: BUTTERFLY NEBULA
         NASA, www.nasa.gov

PAGE 6, photo: FROZEN LAKE
         PUBLIC DOMAIN, www.public-domain-images.com

PAGE 12, photo: SNOWFLAKE (electron microscope) USDA,
         WIKIMEDIA COMMONS , www.commons.wikimedia.com

PAGE 13, photo: STARS
         NASA, www.nasa.gov

PAGE 16, photo: SWALLOWTAIL BUTTERFLY
         PUBLIC DOMAIN, www.public-domain-images.com

PAGE 18, photo: FROSTED LEAVES
         SARAH SMITH , www.commons.wikimedia.com

PAGE 21, image: DRAGON
         WIKIMEDIA COMMONS , www.commons.wikimedia.com

PAGE 29, photo: FULL MOON
         NASA, www.nasa.gov

PAGE 35, photo: BOBCAT
         PUBLIC DOMAIN, www.public-domain-images.com

PAGE 36, photo: MOONRISE OVER A SEA
         ROB WOUDSMA, www.rwoudsma@live.ca

www.ingramcontent.com/pod-product-compliance
Lightning Source LLC
Chambersburg PA
CBHW060849270326
41934CB00002B/58